MADISON TITUS

The Little Book of Big Conversations

Beginner's Guide to Asking Extraordinary Questions

Curiosity is the one thing invincible in
Nature.

Freya Stark

Contents

1

Introduction

Child-like curiosity can and will change your life for the better. Remember back when you were a kid? Imagine how much different life would be if you chose to see the world through the lens of a child again. Our perception of the world around us is what creates our reality, not reality itself. Just by responding to your environment in a curious way, rather than an assumptive reaction, you have the power to completely alter your experience of reality. Children question everything. Not in a rude way, but because they want to *understand*. If we tried to understand before making assumptions, we would be much happier human beings. If we didn't take life for face value, but instead asked questions to learn more and see things from multiple perspectives, then we would realize we are the creators of our own reality.

I realized in my adolescence the easiest way to practice curiosity was by asking people questions. It started out as a playful act, asking silly questions and making people giggle. Then it became more serious, as I noticed the power of connection I held just by asking deeper questions. Then it became my identity. My mission. I wanted to be unforgettable.

I wanted people to be able to leave an interaction with me and think, "wow, I really like the way she just made me feel." It didn't take long for me to realize the simple act of asking someone a question and allowing them to feel seen, heard, and understood, could set me apart from 99% of the population. So in a world of conforming, average individuals, I found my superpower and no one could take it away from me.

I now pass my superpower onto you. In the pages ahead, I will explain how questions have led to deep conversations, and those deep conversations have led to the most profound relationships, connections, and opportunities in my life. This will include specific questions I enjoy asking and why. Oh, and use your new powers wisely. Let's jump right in!

2

Importance of Genuine Curiosity

Question Everything - Never Stop Learning

You don't have to be a conspiracy theorist to question everything. Actually, I highly recommend doing it for the next month and watch how life unfolds itself right in front of your eyes. When you ask questions, you get answers. When you seek for answers, you start finding gaps in your current belief system or reality. I encourage you to be exhilarated when you find holes in your boat. It means you are no longer accepting life for face value, which is rarely accurate anyway. Genuine curiosity allows you to go down rabbit holes you didn't even know existed. We can't choose where we grew up, who our parents are, or what social class we were raised in. We can't control the religion or belief system we were subconsciously adopted into as a kid.

But, here's the beautiful thing about the world we live in… we have the ability to not believe everything we are taught. Thanks to modern day technology, we have access to education to expand our knowledge. Once you're old enough to be independent and spread your wings, I highly encourage everyone to live somewhere else for a few years. Life is so much more expansive than your current circumstances. Being open-minded is the first step to changing the lens in which you see the world. Be open to the fact that your current situation is not the ultimate truth. Question what your parents told you. Question what your teachers told you. Question what society told you to do or who to be. Question what success really means. Question what happiness is. Question what love looks like and feels like. Question the value of money. Question your parents' relationship with money. Question your relationship with money. Question why you listen to the music you like. Question how you and your best friend met. Question your favorite food. Question your favorite color. Question what you want to be when you grow up.

I could go on forever on all the things you should be questioning. Life isn't always black or white. In fact, life isn't even that serious. How do I know? Because you could start forming vastly different opinions tomorrow and live an entirely different reality, with very little repercussions. It doesn't matter. We put so much pressure on ourselves to be "perfect" or achieve these high standards; or worse, make our parents proud of us. As if some external job or salary is what's really going to give us the love and approval we're deeply searching for. I challenge you to start wondering why…. Why do we care so much what others think of us? Why do we let money run the world? Why do we believe everything we're told as a child? Why do we believe a guidance counselor can help us decide what we should be when we grow up? Why is envy going to be the achilles heel of our generation? These are the questions to help you not take life so seriously. Because it's not. The second you start questioning everything, the second you realize there is no ultimate truth. There is no "right way" or "wrong way" to live your life. Once you realize this, then you become the creator of your own reality. This is when life starts getting really exciting. Pick your character and start playing!

Active Listening - Embracing Empathy

Active listening in simple terms means you are listening to understand, not to respond. When you ask someone a question, just shut up and listen. Really listen to them. Hear the excitement or pain in their voice. Digest the words that are coming out of their mouth and what it means to them. Try to see it from their perspective and put yourself in their shoes. Imagine what it's like to walk in their shoes and then think about what it would *feel* like. Now we are getting in touch with our empathy. Empathy is recognizing someone's human condition. Empathy is how you create meaningful connections for sustainability and longevity. This is the simplest and easiest way to connect with people on a deeper level, yet so few of us are able to do it. Why? I believe it requires a skillset most people don't have: effort, intention, emotional intelligence, awareness, and unselfishness.

Active listening is listening with intention and purpose. When we have genuine curiosity and ask someone questions, it gives us the ability to exercise our active listening skills. Let's say we have two people, Bob and Sally. Bob asks me a question, then intently listens to my answer and responds accordingly by asking deeper questions. Sally, on the other hand, asks me a question, then half-listens to what I have to say and responds with something relating back to her. Out of those two people, which one do you think made me feel more positive emotions? Which person do you think I would more likely want another interaction with? If you said Bob, you're correct. There's a big difference between asking someone a question and not really caring about the answer vs. giving your full attention.

The questions I teach you to ask don't have as powerful of an effect if you don't care to listen to the answers. Being inquisitive is only impactful if you are enthralled to absorb the answers to come. Active listening, when mastered, can give you insight into a person's soul and cultivate mutual understanding. When you are listening to someone, make sure you're paying attention to their verbal and nonverbal cues. Notice when their tone of voice changes. Read their facial expressions as they talk. Become aware when their body shifts or they get uncomfortable. Look into their eyes when they are speaking to you. Energy does not lie. If you notice they have a heightened voice, raised eyebrows, more opened eyes, and a big smile, they are probably experiencing excitement. In response, nod and smile back at them. Acknowledge how their excitement also awakens excitement within you! Now you both are existing in the same frequency of emotion together, which forms a layer of connection. Likewise, if you notice they have a more serious or shaky tone in their voice, furrowed eyebrows, or avoidant eye contact, they are more likely to be experiencing anguish or discomfort. In this situation, respond based on what you feel they need. For example, you might tilt your head slightly to show concern, or nod slowly with kind eyes. By doing so, you allow them to feel they are being heard.

I understand it isn't natural for everyone to be unusually observant of others, but it's something you can practice and get better at over time. Again, empathy is recognizing someone's human condition. Usually empathizing involves a shared perspective, feeling or emotion between two people. Some individuals are naturally very empathetic, while for others it requires more effort. But I promise you, if you work on your ability to connect with others, it will enhance every aspect of your life. If you are able to feel with others, care about their well-being, and act with compassion, the relationships in your life will drastically increase in value.

Become Well-Liked

Growing up, I didn't like sharing information about myself to others. I didn't like the idea of everyone knowing my personal business. Good news or bad news. I always found something special about keeping it to myself, as if it was some sort of humbling act or saving the burden from others. As a subconscious avoidance tactic, I would ask other people a million questions about themselves to avoid the topic of conversation being on me. As you can imagine, I got really, really good at asking questions. I learned the more engrossed I became in someone else's story, the more pleasant feelings they would associate me with. At first, I didn't understand why friends or family always wanted to spend more time with me. I didn't understand why it was so easy for me to make friends or why I had no enemies. I didn't realize that it was unusual to effortlessly get along with anyone at any age, almost instantaneously. At this point in my life, I didn't comprehend the psychology behind how much people love talking about themselves. Turns out, from a very young age, I had been subconsciously influencing others to like me and crave my presence simply by deflecting questions away from me and asking them more questions about themselves. Wow.

Fast forward a few years and life experiences later, I am an adult in my mid-20's. I've become quite fascinated with human psychology, self-development, relationships, and emotional intelligence. I've read countless books and listened to a healthy amount of podcasts on these topics. All to say, I understand the power I hold now. Not only what to do, but also how to harness it and why it's so important.

The easiest way to get someone to like you is by asking them about themselves. As humans, we LOVE talking about ourselves. It's our favorite topic we could go on and on about. It's the one book where we know all the ins and outs to every chapter. Do you know what's even better than talking about yourself? Someone on the other end who is actually listening and enjoys hearing about your life. You automatically feel cared for and appreciated by someone who listens to you talk about your favorite topic. By asking another person a deep question, you are actively trying to get to know them. Emotional effort in today's society does not go unnoticed. The quickest way to be the most interesting person in the room is by being the most interested in what others have to say.

Now let's take things a step further. If you want people to *really* like you, start cultivating an empathetic connection as they tell you their story. Try to see from their perspective and imagine how they felt in those moments, or even how they feel right now in this present moment. Once you learn to develop compassion for others while they are sharing the most intimate thoughts of their brain with you, then you will become *magnetic*. People will feel such a deep, emotional bond with you and not even be able to comprehend how it happened. All they know is they love the way you make them feel. Being around you is a slice of heaven.

Find your Truth

This power does not come easily. It can be fairly exhausting to emotionally connect with someone. Especially if you do this multiple times a day. You must learn how to protect yourself and your energy, or else you will be exhausted. Sometimes, you get so deep in empathizing with someone, you begin to feel their emotions on such a profound level. Once you get to this point, it can be difficult to release. Use this practice to experience deeper human connection, but not at the sacrifice of your own well-being. Above all else, stay authentic and protect your boundaries.

The reason genuine curiosity plays such an important role in finding your truth is it opens up opportunities and pathways you might not have known otherwise. Once you start questioning everything, you realize you don't really know who you are. Or worse, you don't know what you really want. It's okay to be curious about life; past, present and future. It's okay to be an adult and still question what you want to be when you grow up. There is something so beautiful about someone finding their purpose in life by going outside of their current parameters. I resonate with the famous Socrates quote saying, "all I know, is that I know nothing." The more you learn, grow and evolve, the more you realize there is so much you don't know. I challenge you to expand outside your circumstances, whether it be moving to a new city, experiencing other cultures, or researching differing opinions from the ones you were raised with. Become your own person, with your own opinions and fascinations! Keep an open mind when you are asking other people questions, because they just might alter your concept of reality.

Once you start living your truth by finding your purpose, then you will have incredible answers in return to the questions you are asking others. Maintaining a receptive approach in these deep conversations has expedited my personal journey to self-discovery. Cheers to the ongoing evolution of discovering our truest selves.

3

Questions to Ask Friends

- When was the last time you cried? How come?
- What is something you wished more people asked you about?
- What is a topic you could speak on for an hour with absolutely no preparation?
- If you had to pick one year of your life to relive exactly as it was, which year would you pick?
- If you woke up tomorrow and you had everything you've ever wanted, what would you spend the rest of your life doing?
- What's something you spend way too much time doing?
- What do you think is the biggest misconception people have about you?
- What is something about yourself that sounds made up but is 100% true?
- What's something you would try if no one in the world could judge you?
- What are you most excited for in the future?
- Do you live your life attaining pleasure or avoiding pain more?
- What's something in your life you consider a miracle?

- What is your go-to coping mechanism when life gets hard?
- How would you describe your childhood in 3 words?
- If you had a blank canvas in front of you, what would you draw to reflect your current state of mind?
- What invention do you hope to witness in this lifetime?
- What snack did you eat as soon as you got home from school when you were a kid?
- What is your definition of a best friend?
- Who do you love most in life and why?
- What is something you have been told that you will never forget?
- What is one experience you would want to relive over again?
- Describe your worst heartbreak. What did it teach you?
- What's something normal to you that others find weird?
- If you had to introduce yourself to someone without using your name, age, occupation, ethnicity, or location… how would you describe yourself?
- Who's your go to music artist when you're feeling down?
- What's the first thing you think of when you say "i love ____"?
- What are you currently working on that you're excited about?
- What would you do if you had enough money to not need a job?
- What would you like to change about your life?
- If I was to disappear, what would you remember most about me?
- Who do you feel like really has your back?
- What's an experience that taught you a lot about yourself?
- What color are you feeling right now?
- Do you remember the first time you saw your parents cry?
- Who has influenced the way you think the most?

4

Questions to Ask a Significant Other

- What makes you feel important? What makes you feel seen?
- What makes you feel connected?
- Who is the first person you go to to share good news or celebrate a win?
- When do you feel most like yourself?
- What is something that keeps you up at night?
- What is the best part about being you?
- Do you feel like you are in, approaching, or past your prime?
- What is your biggest fear for the future?
- What does living the "good life" mean to you?
- What makes you fall in love with a person first?
- What was the biggest plot twist in your life?
- What's the most out of character thing you've done or would like to do?
- What does "I love you" mean to you?
- When you think of your childhood, what shows come to mind?
- What does beautiful mean to you?
- If someone told you they saw me arguing with a stranger on the

street, what would you immediately assume I was arguing with them about?

- What few ideas of common sense do you wish the whole world had?
- How do you determine whether you can trust somebody?
- Are you holding onto something you need to let go of?
- What's your happy place?
- What are you afraid of passing down to your kids?
- What's a song you play by yourself but never with other people?
- What's something simple that makes you smile?
- What's something meaningful to you, but not to others?
- What is a tough thing you've dealt with in your past?
- If you could meet anyone, dead or alive, who would it be?
- Do I still feel like the same person I was when we met?
- What about me have you learned that surprised you?
- What's something I do that feels toxic?
- How can I support you into becoming the person you want to be?
- Is there a mistake you felt like you needed to make to become the person you are today?
- What's an experience that left you feeling humbled?
- What's a personal value you will never compromise on?
- When did you last feel proud of your parents?
- What would you change about the way you were raised?
- What emotion do you struggle to deal with?
- What are you most grateful for in this relationship?
- What's a red flag you've ignored before?

5

Questions to Ask Parents

- Before I was born, what were your happiest years or moments?
- What was something you had a hard time getting mad at me for because you also did as a kid?
- What's a quality I have that reminds me of you?
- What are your core memories as a kid?
- What is something you wish more people knew about you?
- What is a decision you made that impacted the trajectory of your life significantly and you didn't realize it at the time?
- Describe what home feels like to you.
- What is the best thing you've ever wanted to quit?
- Are there any apologies you are still waiting for and/or is there anyone you still owe an apology to?
- What should be required reading for every human?
- What do you know, for sure, to be true?
- If you got to go back in time 10-15 years, how would you prove to people that you're from the future?
- Who's the most fascinating person you've met in your life?
- What makes you proud?

- What makes someone a good person?
- What is the most grand gesture of kindness you have ever received or witnessed?
- What chance are you most grateful for taking in this life?
- What everyday simplicities make you nostalgic?
- What's something you've experienced that changed you for the worst? For the better?
- What's a recent realization you've had?
- What do you owe yourself?
- What are you afraid to let go of?
- If you could bring someone back, who would it be and why?
- What is one thing you would change about society?
- What's a memory you never want to let go of?
- What's something you love to do?
- What's something you wish you knew more about?
- If you won the lottery what would you spend your money on?
- What's the most spontaneous thing you've ever done?
- What do you think is my defining trait?
- When was the first time you stood up for something you truly believed in?
- What's a dream or goal you've never shared with anyone else?
- Who encourages you to be the best version of yourself?
- What are you struggling with that I don't know about?
- What do you do to celebrate the good things in your life?
- What do you think is the greatest album of all time?
- What is your favorite concert you've ever been to?

6

Questions to Ask Yourself

- What is a goal you used to have that you look back on now and no longer feel any alignment with?
- What is a flaw that you are aware that you have that you are working on and one that you have no interest in working on at this time?
- What is a skill you have today that you didn't have a year ago?
- What is one intentional thing you do every single day?
- What gets you out of bed in the morning?
- What would the younger version of you not believe about your life today?
- Are you trying to achieve greatness or are you trying to avoid disappointment?
- Is there someone you consider to be your greatest teacher?
- How do you define your authentic self?
- What does your voice of intuition sound like and when was the last time you followed it?
- What promises have you currently made for yourself or others?
- What is the most painful thing you've been told?
- What excuses do you make that hold you back?

- If you could compliment yourself, what would you say?
- When do you feel most at peace?
- Are you happy?
- Who are you?
- Who do you want to be?
- What is occupying your thoughts most at the moment?
- Is there a single moment or experience that changed your life?
- Do you feel like you have enough love in your life?
- Do you think anyone resents you?
- When did you last feel like someone believed in you?
- How do you know if you trust someone?
- Who makes you feel like the best version of yourself?
- Describe a time you found beauty somewhere unexpected.
- What's a moment when you felt your personal growth was recognized by someone else?
- What's a time you had to rely on your intuition?
- What's an experience that's broadened your perspective in a big way?
- What does home feel like for you?
- How do you measure a successful life?
- Who in your life do you think knows you the best?
- What's something you couldn't forgive someone for?
- Has anybody seen you at your worst? What did they do?
- When in your life were you the happiest?
- Who did you allow into your life that you shouldn't have?
- What was an unexpected blessing this year?
- How were you hurt this year? How did you heal?
- Where in the world do you want to travel most?

7

Conclusion

There you have it! All of my favorite questions to start deeper conversations. I hope you enjoyed these questions and share them with your most loved ones. In a world of technology where we're always on our phones, try whipping out some of these questions next time you're around family or friends. You might be surprised by how much you learn not only about them, but also about yourself. Embrace the amazing conversations and connections to come!

If you found this book helpful, I'd be very appreciative if you left a favorable review for the book on Amazon!

www.ingramcontent.com/pod-product-compliance
Lightning Source LLC
Chambersburg PA
CBHW060851260726

48661CB00002B/730